WELCOME TO MEMORY LANE

VOL. 1

RICHMOND, VA

Presented by

K L E O S
INTERNATIONAL, INC.

P.O. Box 386
Richmond, VA 23218
phone (804) 559-9220
fax (804) 559-9221
www.kleosmagazine.com

"Memory Lane, Richmond, VA"
ISBN-10: 1-928662-93-5
ISBN-13: 978-1-928662-93-8

Design and Layout by Landis Productions LLC

Printed by Worth Higgins & Associates, Inc.

Written by R. David Ross

Dedicated to Dolores and Ed Ross

~~~~~~~~~~~~~~~~~~~~~~~~~~~~~~~~~~~~~

A portion of the proceeds of this book
is being donated to the
Community Ideas' Station's "Virginia Currents."

Introduction

My introductory letter in a recent issue of KLEOS Magazine of Richmond used the analogy of a rearview mirror, moving through life and experiencing progress while at the same time looking back to remember where we have been. I've put together a few vignettes of our favorite places that are no longer with us. Places that many of you will fondly remember from yesteryear, your childhood, or even hearing about from loved ones. I've had a lot of fun remembering these Richmond institutions and former landmarks and hope that you will enjoy them as much as I have. Please join me as we walk down *"Memory Lane…"*

– R. David Ross

Table of Contents

Shopped Till We Dropped...

Bounded by Brook Road, Azalea Avenue and Westbrook Avenue was the place so many of us went to shop, grab a bite to eat or have good ol' fun. Woolco and Woolworth's had all the merchandise we needed, from clothes to housewares to tools to lunch counters. The much-beloved Thalhimer's-Azalea was the place for wedding registry, clothing, and silver and china patterns. Gary's for greeting cards, Food Fair for groceries and children's rides for a quarter. Who can forget the monkey in the glass cage in the back of Hofheimer's or being dragged through the Mediterranean-style LaVogue for upscale clothing with our mothers? And remember the fun of the twice-yearly petting zoo, where lambs, goats and other animals endured our petting?

And how many of us bought our first girlfriend's or fiancée's jewelry at the locally owned Rees Jewelers? Of course, before shopping, we all went to Bank of Virginia, in the parking lot, to get cash from our very first passbook savings account.

The days of Azalea Mall may be gone, but those memories will be with us forever.

Do I visit the stores or order from the catalog?

We need a lawnmower…we need a bracelet…we need luggage…we need crystal…we need baseballs and footballs. Where do we go? Best Products. Founded by Richmonders Sydney and Frances Lewis, and headquartered in Richmond, the once catalog-based company was where we went, either physically or through ordering, to purchase virtually anything. A national success story, Best stores were found throughout the entire nation, with many in Richmond. They became known for their eclectic and interesting architecture as much as for their product lines. One store had the front wall "peeling off"; another was made with ceramic tile. The headquarters displayed some of the Lewises' magnificent art collection, so generously shared with all of us. Though a publicly traded company, Best was such a part of our lives, we felt like we were co-owners. Somehow, we believe that is what the Lewises had in mind.

If ever a company was appropriately named, it was Best.

Let's Take the Train!

We traveled for vacations. Executives went up and down the East Coast on business. The sight of the large, round rotunda meant vacation to many, work for some. But to a lot of us, it represented an annual outing that was always more fun than the year before. For the month after Thanksgiving, Broad Street Station was overwhelmed by the smiles on our faces from taking the Santa Claus Train to Washington, D.C. Toys and presents, music, refreshments and fun were all a part of this half-day outing. Santa made each of us feel like we were the only one onboard. The excitement of riding the train, the anticipation of Christmas, the jolliness of Saint Nick, all combined for a wonderful family day. That beautiful train station has become the home of the Science Museum of Virginia and has welcomed hundreds of thousands of visitors in that capacity. We are so fortunate to have retained the glory of that old building.

Santa comes only once a year, but we started looking forward to the Santa Claus Train at summer's end.

It's a Byrd...It's a plane...

We had been bowling recently and had enough of putt-putt. There weren't any good movies playing, and we weren't interested in any television shows. What could we do that would be fun and interesting? What might be different from last week's outings? Going to Byrd Airport to sit in the observation deck and watch the airplanes land and take off. Unencumbered by security and barriers, we went to the airport sometimes just to watch. Other times, we were saying goodbye to a loved one or picking them up from a flight. Regardless, we could go to the observation area, shielded by only half walls of glass, and see everyone boarding and deplaning without jet ways. We would be sitting no more than 100 feet from a Piedmont or Eastern Airlines plane, waving and yelling to our friends or family members. Being a part of aviation was so much more real when practically standing next to the plane. And when it was time for the planes to take off or land, the jet noise was so deafening, yet so exciting, it made us want to be a pilot when we grew up.

No one will ever deny that the success of Richmond International Airport, formerly Byrd Airport, is the ultimate progress. But we do miss seeing and hearing the jets and loved ones so close we could touch them.

Going, going, GONE!

Summer would wind down and school would begin. Warm weather activities stopped, and we often retreated to the family television set after dinner. A sitcom? A nighttime soap opera? A weekly whodunit series? For nine nights per year, the television was more likely tuned to WCVE for Channel 23's Great TV Auction. The station's largest annual fundraiser was as much a shopathon as it was philanthropy. Items donated by local businesses and residents were shown, and we excitedly called in to place our bids. Each "area" and its items would be shown 2 or 3 times, and we would watch intently as the items' bids went higher. Sporting goods, household appliances and decorative items were sold through phones manned by well-trained volunteers. And the more expensive items, such as the occasional boat, car or Cybis porcelain sculpture were sold live, by Bob Jones – auctioneer, with callers staying on the phone as they bid. The entire family joined in the excitement.

Online auctions and Internet buying may be convenient, but they are nowhere near as exciting as Channel 23's Great TV Auction.

I've Been Working on the Railroad

Richmond's rail system was more extensive in bygone years than it is today. Broad Street Station and Main Street Station were popular for passenger travel. Even more important, goods and products were transported by rail via the region's vast railroad system. One sight became more familiar to us than the proverbial caboose or engineer: a cat. On the side of at least one car of virtually every freight train owned and operated by the Chesapeake & Ohio Railroad was the familiar image of the same sleeping cat. He also appeared on household items made for promotional purposes—playing cards, matches, drinking glasses, buttons, bags and too many others to name. Who was this feline friend so familiar to all of us? His name was Chessie. C&O adopted Chessie as its mascot, and the image of the sleeping animal became part of its logo and image. We all considered him ours, and his likeness appeared on any number of items in our home. Sure, we had our household pets. But the faces of kids of all ages lit up when Chessie was nearby.

Chesapeake & Ohio grew and merged and became even more important to our area's corporate successes. But we still think so fondly of our beloved Chessie.

Hmm...Where should we go for ice cream?

That was a question not asked much as we grew up because we knew where we would go. Where did we always gather after Cotillion, school dances and festivals for ice cream and socializing? The Clover Room. Famous for their hot fudge sundaes and banana splits, the Clover Room was the site for gathering after almost any nighttime function. From the tables for two, where couples on dates sat, to seating for 25, where a group would congregate from one of the evening's festivities, we all knew where we would go, what we would have, and with whom we would sit. And if you wanted to enjoy a treat for later, you could take your ice cream home in one of their famous orange Clover Room to-go containers, emblazoned with the green three-leaf clover. What great nights we had with our friends and family, reliving all the important events.

Sure, there are chains where we get our ice cream now...but there will never be another Clover Room.

Where is our most famous musician playing today?

Will we hear him today at the Miller & Rhoads tearoom? Or maybe he will play the national anthem tonight at the Richmond Robins game at the Coliseum. Maybe, just maybe, if we are lucky, he will make the Mighty Wurlitzer dance as it rises from the floor of the stage at the Byrd Theater. Who? We didn't have to ask who. We knew it was Eddie Weaver. Present at virtually every major event, festival and venue in the Richmond area, Eddie Weaver played to tens of thousands of us each year in all of the above locations. When we needed someone to provide background music for an event, or deliver a concert to delight all ages and generations, he was the one we called. Dates, parties, recitals, luncheons, teas and countless other functions were made so much more delightful by Eddie Weaver and his magical fingers. If we asked someone else to provide music, he must have been out of town or, more likely, already booked.

Eddie Weaver made us realize organs weren't just for churches.

That Professional Look

We needed suits, blazers and slacks, and we needed them badly. First job interviews, long-term careers, cocktail parties and traveling were all made easier by knowing where to go for the right outfit: Jefferson Men's Clothing. For the right "Richmond look," the Nachman family would size us up as we walked in the door and have us in the right area of the store before we could ask for help. Located in a barebones building on Marshall Street, it was the site of many sales, fashion shifts and outfitting of happy gatherings. The store then took the bold move of relocating to Short Pump in an upscale store. Who can forget the famous radio commercials— "This is Rosa Lee Nachman for Lady Jefferson"—as they introduced their line of women's clothing. Ultrasuede and tweed were the order of the day. We went with our entire families, knowing we would get the right clothing sold by the right people.

Ordering clothes online? Madison Avenue? We were happy with Jefferson.

Hotel John Marshall, Richmond, Virginia

EL JOHN MARSHALL
RICHMOND, VIRGINIA

For Classy Events...

Where did so many proms, weddings and galas take place while we were growing up and entering adulthood? The John Marshall Hotel, located between 7th and 8th streets, and Franklin and Grace streets, was the site of many affairs. High schools used the elegant grand ballroom for teenagers' first formal events. The Tobacco Festival Ball was held there each fall. So many weddings and receptions were staged in the setting etched in our minds. Students attended conventions at the John Marshall, from the Key Club convention, to Boys' and Girls' State. And if you needed to primp before any event, you could always get your hair cut in the basement barber shop.

The future of this grand old property remains uncertain. But many of us will remember it as the site of our first black-tie event and where we learned to use the proper fork.

Let's go see a movie in style.

Seeing a movie in the Richmond area was a different experience decades ago. The setting for our own, our parents' and our grandparents' dates was different from modern movie theaters. Elegance, ornate décor and varied entertainment are what movie-goers expected—and got. Where did we go for such great times? The Loew's Theater on Grace Street. Loew's opened with much fanfare on April 9, 1928, when Governor Harry Byrd attended the silent film "West Point," starring Joan Crawford. For decades, MGM and United Artists films were screened there. Eddie Weaver, master of the Mighty Wurlitzer, played four shows a day there. Local radio and television legend Harvey Hudson broadcast his radio live on the sidewalk in front of Loew's. The theater continued to be a hub of activity for decades, until closing in 1979. Remaining dark until 1983, this grand old place reopened as the Carpenter Center for the Performing Arts.

Cable and DVDs have their advantages, but there was nothing like seeing a movie at Loew's.

A gown for the Bal du Bois or wedding?

Where did our mothers, sisters, neighbors and friends go for that perfect dress for *the* wedding? Which ladies' clothing store clad more women for Richmond's Bal du Bois than any other? Where could the simple "little black dress" or the designer beaded gown be purchased? Montaldo's, of course. Located in downtown Richmond, and later in the River Road Shopping Center, this store was known for its "perfect look" evening dresses, women's suits and wedding dresses, and carried all the accessories to make that event perfect. For years, countless husbands, boyfriends and fiances paced the floors and sidewalks, waiting for "just the right one" to be found. Sure to see neighbors and friends shopping for the same event, we were certain to find the perfect outfit that was one-of-a-kind, so we would not see a mirror image of ourselves across the dance floor. Montaldo's added as much elegance to events as any planner or florist.

International chain stores did not stand a chance when Montaldo's doors were open.

How about a bagel and some lox?

When we craved a true deli-style meal, we knew where to go without a second thought. Eggs, lox and bagels for breakfast—not a problem. A sailor sandwich, reuben or hot dog with sauerkraut and chili, New York style? We all went to the famous New York Deli on West Cary Street in Carytown. With the perfect dose of great food and 1950s-style vinyl booths, tables and tablecloths, any time was the perfect time for a kosher meal or favorite sandwich. And on the left-hand side of the store, as we entered and exited, we passed the refrigerated containers of meats, cheeses, breads, condiments, and all the other ingredients necessary for Richmond's true deli experience. As much food was carried out for at-home meals and parties as was eaten on site. The restaurant recently was sold, renovated and reopened as an upscale restaurant, bar and club. Nighttime bar business is as much a focus now as corned beef and pastrami was then.

We still can get a few of the traditional items at the new New York Deli, but we sure do miss those vinyl booths and kitschy décor.

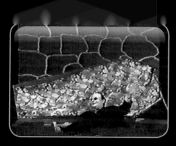

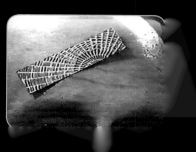

Furniture shopping by day? Shock Theatre by night?

We need a new bedroom set and a new sofa for the family room. The porch furniture is rusted and two kitchen chairs broken. Where should we go to fill all these needs? Popkin Furniture. Oddly enough, their number-one salesperson and spokesman was none other than Bowman Body. A strangely friendly ghost/vampire who never scared a soul, Bowman Body was a household name because of the many television, radio and newspaper advertisements he was featured in. As bizarre as his selection as a spokesperson was the affection we all had for him. The furniture was, of course, good quality. But it seemed Bowman Body was just as responsible for attracting customers as the many sofas, chairs and beds themselves. Located at Jefferson and East Broad streets, the building is now an upscale restaurant and bar called Popkin Tavern. Though wonderfully renovated, the building still boasts features such as the original pressed-tin ceiling. And the specialty of the house? The Bowman Burger.

We would all love to see that friendly ghost again.

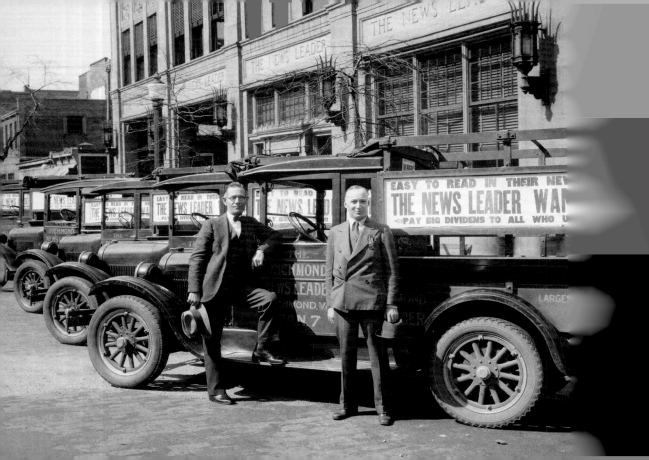

When is that newspaper coming?

About 2:30 in the afternoon, we all would check our watches and clocks to see how long before it would come. What had happened in the last 12 or so hours? What exciting news would we find out about? Who did what, and when? And then it came…the Richmond News Leader. Long the afternoon paper in the Richmond area, it covered what had happened since the printing of the Richmond Times-Dispatch late the night before. Of course, these were fondly referred to as the "morning paper" and the "afternoon paper." In addition to the latest news, we could always count on human interest stories, household hints, wedding announcements and the ultra-important column on Thursdays and Saturdays: "The Whirl of Richmond." Written by Charlotte Taylor Massie, this column was the who-what-when of Richmond society. We had to know who was visiting whom, what functions were held and where they were. Hard news was important, but it got read after the important stuff.

Even with all the access to real-time news at our fingertips today, so many of us still look at our watches about 2:30 in the afternoon.

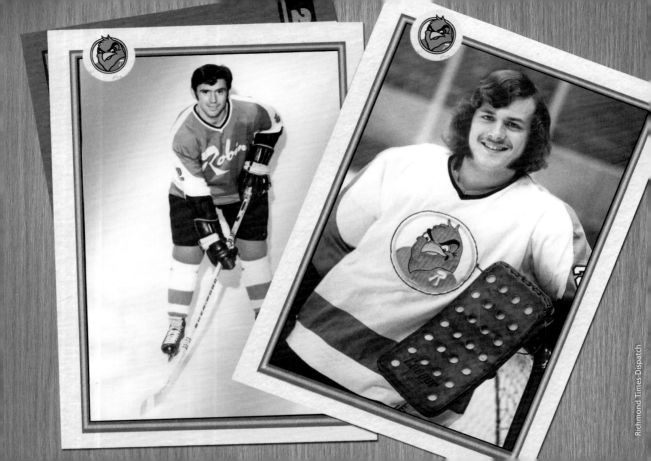

"All the little birdies go tweet tweet tweet."

When we heard those words echoing through the rafters of the Richmond Coliseum, we knew what was to come. The excitement of one of the greatest Richmond traditions was about to begin. The team theme song meant that the players were coming out, and we were about to watch our heroes—the Richmond Robins—in action. All the fans sang the words to "Rockin' Robin" and then we quieted down for the national anthem. From that point on, it was a toss-up as to who was actually watching the hockey game and who was hoping for the next fight. No doubt the fights were all part of the drama the fans sought. But couple that with a hot dog and fries, and a hockey game with friends, in a venue that held over 10,000 fans, and we knew we would be checking the schedule for the next game.

We have great professional sports teams now, including hockey. But we sure did love our Robins.

How many more books do we need to fill?

Remember those little sheets of stamps we were given when we would check out of various retail stores? The number of sheets was determined by the total purchases at the store. What do we do with them? What *are* they? S&H Greenstamps. So many nights, we sat down with our families, applying our amassed sheets of S&H Greenstamps to the pages of the empty booklets provided to us. All the while, we would be eyeing the redemption catalog for what we wanted to eventually purchase. Did we want a family item like a household appliance? Or maybe sports

equipment? Did we want to get that coveted Carrom Board, with 22 games all in one? Over time, maybe we could get them all! And interestingly, collecting the stamps, filling the books and anticipating the reward became as much fun as actually receiving the item itself. So many garages were filled with items obtained with S&H Greenstamps.

We always wanted to spend more to get more stamps, to get that last book filled. Ever wonder where those treasured items are now?

Red Light, Green Light

As kids, we all got carted around by our parents. From infancy to kindergarten, from teenage years to first dates, Mom and Dad were our transportation system. But how could we ever learn what needed to be learned, not just in a vehicle, but when crossing the road and waiting for traffic on neighborhood streets and during outings and field trips? Safety Town was the answer. Located in the parking lot on the south side of Azalea Mall, we could go to this miniature small-scale town to learn traffic rules that would keep us out of harm's way. Whether we were with our families, on class field trips or with friends, the 3-foot-high traffic signs were perfect for us in our early years. Safety became fun. This miniature town was where we learned how to act long before driver's ed was even thought about. Hand signals, traffic lights, intersections and everything else we needed to know was taught in a fun, simple "to-size" manner and place.

Who knows how many of us were saved from accidents because of our beloved Safety Town?

"I'm Popeye the Sailor Man"

Sure, there were Captain Kangaroo, Mr. Green Jeans, Kukla, Fran and Ollie, and the rest. Comics books were for sale on every street corner. National radio and television shows were becoming more popular every month, touting their own cartoon characters and heroes. The challenge of the day was how to entertain and educate children at the same time. And we had our hero, Sailor Bob, who did just that. "The Popeye and Friends Show," broadcast on WRVA-TV (now WWBT TV12), was more than that to us: It was the Sailor Bob show. Complete with his own puppet characters, Sailor Bob made us all watch intently as he would draw additional characters and cartoons between Popeye shows. He would read fan mail that we had sent. If we were lucky enough to have our birthday party celebrated in the studio, or to attend someone else's, we thought we had seen the most importantly celebrity in the world. And imagine our excitement when we saw him in the Better Living Building or on the midway of the state fair, drawing for us.

Cable cartoon shows and characters may play round the clock, but it was more exciting to sit by the television and wait for the morning or afternoon Sailor Bob show.

Dancing to Big Band Music

Where did we go when we wanted a night out of music, dancing, conversation and friends? What place was a combination of class, relaxation, revelry and memories? Where was it simply assumed we were going on New Year's Eve? Tantilla Garden, located at Hamilton and Broad streets. Cocktail dresses and pearls for women and suits for men were the uniforms of the day. In an era before liquor by the drink, if we wanted adult refreshments, we took a brown paper bag. When ready for another beverage, we turned the lid on the gas table lantern, so the waitress knew it was time for a refill. Echoes of Les Brown, Tommy Dorsey, Guy Lombardo and the like filled the air. And if we decided we had danced enough or wanted more casual entertainment, we could go bowling at Tiny Town, located downstairs.

Sadly for us, Tantilla Garden closed in 1969. They sure don't make entertainment complexes like that anymore.

Visit Us
CHESTERFIELD'S
GREAT MODERN
FACTORY
6th & Cary

CHESTERFIELD

CHESTERFIELD

Chesterfield
CIGARETTES

Dementi

Sitting along Broad Street wrapped in blankets

Late afternoon on a Friday in fall, we all started to gather along West Broad Street. We arrived as early as possible to get the best spot. Businesses closed early so their employees and their families could set up chairs in their parking lots from a prime vantage point. As time got near, the crowds were dozens deep, growing to over 100,000. What were we waiting for? The Tobacco Festival Parade. The culmination of a number of Tobacco Festival events, the parade was eagerly anticipated by all of us throughout the year. Scores of high school bands practiced tirelessly all season for their marching appearance in the annual parade. A Hollywood star served as grand marshal. Shriners were peppered throughout, from the marching chanters, to the miniature race cars, to the antique vehicles. 4-H clubs, cheerleaders, corporate and organization floats, and countless others paraded down West Broad Street over a period of two to three hours, delighting everyone in their path. And who could forget the Ferko String Band, those famous Mummers from Philadelphia?

We all understood the sentiment from the song "I Love a Parade."

Where should we go for dinner after prom?

It's prom night and we want to impress our date. Where do we go for dinner? It's time to "pop the question" and we wanted the right setting with the perfect view. Where do we take such an important step? It's time to celebrate another anniversary, birthday, graduation or another of life's milestones. What is the perfect place? The Top of the Tower Restaurant. Located on West Franklin Street on the top level of the Lexington Towers Apartment Building, the Top of the Tower was one of the places we chose to celebrate, impress and wine-and-dine. With an elegant décor, varied menu and one of the best views of the city, especially at night, it's no wonder we chose this fine dining establishment for so many evenings out. Romance, music and candlelight were the order of the day. And we knew we could expect that, and more, at the Top of the Tower.

Proms were much less nerve-racking because we knew where we would have dinner with our dates.

VIRGINIA

SA

"Milk and cookies anyone?"

We needed milk to start the day off. Recipes called for whole milk, buttermilk, or sour cream. Health conscious households used cottage cheese as a staple. All these dairy products filled our refrigerators, and remarkably, arrived without a trip to the grocery store. But, where did they come from? Who could we count on to make sure we had these regularly used wholesome products? Virginia Dairy. Though located on Main Street, Virginia Dairy, owned and operated by the civic-minded Rennie family, delivered these and a number of other dairy products to our homes. The milk came in the recognizable glass bottles with the "bubble" that collected the cream. It also was packaged in cardboard containers that could be used as coin banks to save our pocket change.

Other products came in similarly familiar containers, all emblazoned with the Virginia Dairy logo. When we ran out of the products, we knew the Virginia Dairy trucks would be through our neighborhoods to replenish our stock…and take the empty bottles we had left in the metal carrying cases we had been furnished for safe storage.

Who would make it their business to make sure we had all that we need in the icebox and then refrigerator? Virginia Dairy.

Alcohol 62 to 68 Per Cent

DOSE: 30 to 60 drops in a little water in
treatment of Nausea, Faintness or Acid
the Stomach.

Net   Fl. Ozs.

WILLEY DRUG COMPANY
Phone 5-4395

1205 Bellevue Ave.,   RICHMOND

Limeade, anyone?

If we lived in Northside—or drove through, knew anyone who lived in or ever visited Northside—then we knew where to get the best limeade in town: Willey's Drug. Located on Bellevue Avenue in the Bellevue section of town, and across from the Ginter Park area, Willey's was where we all purchased our sundries and cosmetics, got our prescriptions filled and had refreshments at the counter. Whether for adults after work or children after school, it was a safe haven to meet, enjoy and shop. And the mainstay for whom the pharmacy was named? Pharmacist Edward E. Willey Sr. As he filled prescriptions and dished out advice to customers, one would never suspect he was one of the most powerful and influential figures in Virginia history. The senior state senator from Richmond for over three decades, he was chairman of the powerful Senate Finance Committee, responsible for the funding of all projects. This quiet, firm man embodied all that was good of that era, in the political, business and medical arenas.

Many think a drugstore is a drugstore is a drugstore...clearly, they never visited Willey's.

Where does everyone want to go for lunch?

It's midday and we are hungry. Soup? Salad? What does everyone want? Wait—how 'bout Chicken-in-the-Rough? Well, that answered that. We all wanted to go to Wright's Townhouse, at the corner of Azalea Avenue and Brook Road. Boasting country décor, of course Wright's Townhouse had a full menu. But the chicken, posted proudly on the outside marquis, was its signature meal. Businessmen dropped by for lunch. Ladies had their luncheon meetings there. Families stopped in for dinner. No question, you would run into fellow swim team members, buddies from school, neighbors and fellow churchgoers. Wright's Townhouse was one of our beloved hangouts. The food, the friendliness of the owners, and the at-home feeling made it a place to visit at least weekly. And the pies…oh, the pies.

Long before the days of everything being grilled and the fear of trans fats, there was Chicken in the Rough. To have it one more time…

Do you need additional copies of *"Memory Lane"* to share with friends and family? Keep a sharp eye out for them at local retailers or visit www.kleosmagazine.com to order copies online.

Are you a big fan of a Richmond landmark we missed in Volume One? Send a letter to KLEOS International, Inc., P.O. Box 386, Richmond, VA 23218 or visit www.kleosmagazine.com today to suggest entries for future volumes of *"Memory Lane."*

Special thanks to: Joe Brooks, Roy & Emily Putze, Christina K. Garrett, Whiting's Old Paper, Bill Bowman, John D. Clarke and Twyla Kulp.